One World:
Sociology & Funeral Service

Funeral Service Education Resource Center

FSERC

Dedicated to the Advancement of Funeral
Service Education

John B. Fritch, Ph.D. &
Gary Steward Jr., Ph.D.

Funeral Service Education Resource Center
12316A North May Avenue, Suite #209
Oklahoma City, OK 73120

First Publication 2016, Printed in the U.S.A.

ISBN: 978-0-692-67592-2

Published by The:
Funeral Service Education Resource Center
12316-A North May Avenue, Suite #209
Oklahoma City, Oklahoma 73120
Phone: 405-226-3155
Email: fnrleducation@gmail.com
Website: www.fserc.com

John B. Fritch, Ph.D.

Dr. Fritch holds a B.A. in Economics from the University of Kansas, a B.S. in Funeral Service from the University of Central Oklahoma, an M.Ed. also from the University of Central Oklahoma, and a Doctor of Philosophy specializing in Higher Education Leadership and Policy Studies from Oklahoma State University. He is also a licensed funeral director, embalmer, and certified crematory operator.

Fritch is the chairperson for the University of Central Oklahoma Department of Funeral Service Education. Although his full-time position at the university demands the majority of his time, he has remained committed to staying current in the funeral service profession and continues to practice as a funeral director and embalmer when possible. His research focus centers on quality funeral service education and what elements define such classification. In addition to his leadership role at Central and practicing as a funeral director and embalmer, he is also the founder of the Funeral Service Education Resource Center, a company dedicated to the advancement of funeral service education. Fritch is also the co-author of Fires of Change: A Comprehensive examination of Cremation, and he also serves as the co-editor of the Journal of Funeral Service Education.

Gary Steward, Jr., Ph.D.

Dr. Steward holds a B.A. in Sociology from Central State University and a M.A. in Criminal Justice Management and Administration from the University of Central Oklahoma. He earned his doctoral degree (sociology) in 1999 from Oklahoma State University.

Dr. Steward is the Associate Vice President for Institutional Effectiveness at the University of Central Oklahoma (UCO). He has served the university as a faculty member (1997-2005), assistant dean (2004), associate dean for eight years (2005-2012), and dean of the College of Liberal Arts for three years before his current appointment.

Although Dr. Steward has been serving UCO in full-time academic administration since 2005, he continues to teach a variety of courses that have a wide-spread appeal to the broader campus, including the *Sociology of Death and Dying.* His research interests include death and dying, new religious movements, and collective behavior/social movements.

Leslie Similly, Ph.D., Book Editor

Chapter Editors:

Jamye D. Jeter Cameron, MBA, CFSP: Jamye is a native of Detroit, MI, and a third generation funeral director and embalmer. Jamye was the 64th President of the National Funeral Directors and Morticians Association, Inc. She began her teaching career at Wayne State University- Mortuary Science Program in 2006. In 2015, she was hired to serve as the Director of Funeral Service Education at Lake Washington Institute of Technology.

Damon de la Cruz, Ph.D.: Damon, a California licensed embalmer and funeral director is the Funeral Service Education Department Chair at American River College in Sacramento, CA. He holds a B.S. in Cellular and Molecular Biology from California State University, Northridge and a Ph.D. in Pathobiology from the University of Southern California.

Doug Ferrin, M.S.: Doug is the Funeral Service Education Program Director at Mt. Hood Community College. He is a graduate of Dallas Institute of Funeral Service and also holds a B.A. from Colorado State University and an M.S. from Portland State University. He has been actively engaged in the funeral service profession since 1993.

Joseph R. Finocchiaro, CFSP: Joseph is the Program Coordinator of the Funeral Service Education Program at Miami Dade College. He is a passionate funeral service educator and has published articles in both national and state funeral industry publications. He is a member of various professional, fraternal, and philanthropic organizations.

David S. Hess, M.S. Ed.: David is an Assistant Professor and Program Director of the Mortuary Science Program at Salt Lake Community College. He is a graduate of Southern Illinois University earning a Master of Science degree in Education with emphasis on Vocational Education, a Bachelor of Science degree focusing on small business management, and an Associate of Applied Science degree in Mortuary Science and Funeral Service. He has been active in funeral service for over 27 years as a licensed funeral director and embalmer in Illinois, Missouri and Utah.

Images: All images (except chapter 2 cover photo on page 18, this image courtesy of John B. Fritch) in this text, including the cover image, are courtesy of Pixabay.com. All images and videos on Pixabay are released free of copyrights under Creative Commons CC0. You may download, modify, distribute, and use them royalty-free for anything you like, even in commercial applications. Attribution is not required.

This book is dedicated to all funeral service students and educators; your perseverance is our inspiration as we work together for excellence in funeral service education!

Table of Contents

Sociology & Funeral Service: Table of Contents

Foreword

Consistent with the fundamental purpose of the Funeral Service Education Resource Center, the inspiration to publish One World: Sociology & Funeral Service was driven by the reality that a quality text that explores the relationship between sociology and funeral service simply did not exist.

Our dedication to the advancement of Funeral Service Education demanded that we include the expertise of a sociologist in the development and writing of this book. The collaboration between a sociologist and a funeral director delivers a presentation that is both educational and engaging. This book provides the opportunity to explore and learn the essential elements of sociology, while maintaining a profound awareness of the importance to bridge this knowledge with the impact on the funeral service industry.

This text explores the interwoven relationship between funeral service and sociology. Discover the deep connection that exists between these worlds. Read, Learn, and Enjoy!

Introduction

Social life, especially in western cultures, has undergone dramatic changes over the past 50 years. While change is inherent to any social collectivity, past and present, the scope and rapidity of change has accelerated in recent times. There are few places in the United States, if any, that have not been touched by globalization. The appreciation for cultural differences has not been more valued than in contemporary life.

A multicultural community presents opportunities for the funeral service practitioner, but these opportunities, to meet the needs and demands of today's client, require a broader understanding of culture and contextual landscape on the part of the practitioner. Simply stated, understanding the fundamentals of sociology is essential to the funeral service practitioner.

Sociology provides the tools necessary for practitioners to navigate the dramatic cultural changes over the past 50 years. It not only provides the language to contextualize these changes, but also equips the professional with a framework to effectively meet the needs of an increasingly variegated clientele.

Chapter One introduces key ideas embedded in sociology, specifically, the tension and contradiction between social change and social stability or tradition. Additionally, key concepts of the components of culture, building blocks of society, socialization, and the role of rituals are addressed as well. Chapter Two briefly outlines major contributors that have fueled social change. These include broad economic changes manifested in industrialism and post-industrialism, urbanization, the growth of bureaucracies and institutions in terms of breadth and depth, and the impact of greater life expectancy.

Chapter Three connects sociology to the funeral industry by affirming the nature of the funeral ritual as, fundamentally, a social event. The remainder of this chapter describes the centrality of family, in its various forms, to the social ritual of the funerary. In Chapter Four, the impact of institutions, such as the economy and polity (government) are discussed. Demographic factors that affect the funeral industry, such as race/ethnicity, education, and income as well as the impact of social stratification are reviewed. The final chapter (Chapter Five) outlines contemporary trends for the funeral service practitioner. These current trends will provide opportunities as well as challenges to the practitioner.

Chapter One: An Introduction to Sociology

Chapter Editor: Damon de la Cruz, Ph.D.

Chapter 1 Learning Objectives

- Grasp a basic understanding of sociology and how it relates to funeral service.
- Appreciate the relationship between sociology and the evolution of society.
- Understand elements of culture from a sociological perspective; including values, symbols, and norms.
- Develop an appreciation of the building blocks of society, including aspects of roles, statuses, groups, organizations, and institutions.
- Comprehend aspects of socialization.
- Recognize the role of rituals in social life.

~ AN INTRODUCTION TO SOCIOLOGY ~

One of the distinguishing features of modern life is the increasing pace of globalization. Globalization is the process of connecting countries and cultures in economic, political, and social activities. The result of such activities means that disparate cultures are brought together in living patterns that are new and, perhaps, unprecedented. While this text does not specifically address the genesis or a theoretical framework of globalization, the consequences are evident in every corner of social and economic activity, including the American funeral industry.

Forces of globalization have been present since time immemorial. Trading and commerce have driven globalization since the beginning of trade. What distinguishes current trends is the celerity of cultural changes that are unfolding in politics, religion, entertainment, sports, business etc. Collectively, these changes are forging what sociologist refers to as "multicultural" patterns of living. It is commonplace to find cuisines from every continent and region of the world in any U.S. metropolitan area. In fact, it would be unusual and even a pause for curiosity if one could not find specialty shops selling products from all parts of the world.

In addition, many of the goods that are consumed by Americans are produced elsewhere. The idea of an American made car, for example, is no longer a tenable slogan. American car manufacturers import many of the components incorporated in automobiles from "elsewhere". The utensils that we use are most likely produced in foreign countries. How often have you spoken to someone at an outsourced call center who is located outside of the U.S. about your computer, cell phone bill, or customer service? While these examples may seem insignificant to the casual observer, their presence signals something that is much more sociologically important.

Some experts suggest that technology is increasing exponentially. The impact of this increased technology on culture cannot be understated. Modern technological marvels compress the age-old cultural barriers of time and space. Air travel, for example, can move people from one place to the most remote location in the world within a 24 hour period. What required weeks and perhaps months 150 years ago can be accomplished within a day. This mobility creates living patterns that are new to this era of human history. Additionally, advances in communication (internet and television) expose us to disparate cultures and beliefs, with views on life, morality, politics, religion, and death that may be very different than views held by many Americans.

How does globalization impact the funeral industry? Why should the funeral home director be concerned by such matters? What impact does cultural change have on the funeral home? Perhaps most importantly to students of funerary studies is the question; "what is the value of a sociological approach in understanding the important cultural rituals of funeral services?"

A sociological perspective can provide students of the funerary with a set of tools, concepts, or lenses that will help them uncover and understand the dramatic cultural changes that characterize modern life and the corresponding impact on the funeral service industry. Initially, this text will lay the foundation and explain central concepts of the sociological perspective. These include culture, socialization, norms, the building blocks of social life, and the role of rituals in a social context. Next, we will address social factors that bear on funeral service including, family, demographics, religion, urbanization, the economy, and polity.

Building a Foundation

From the earliest days of sociology as a discipline, the founder, August Comte, recognized a universal characteristic of society. He labeled his observation as social statics and social dynamics. He noted that societies contained forces or elements that tended to stabilize and bring order to social life. But Comte also recognized that society was subject to change. Sociological ideas and concepts, in some measure, tease out (intentionally or unintentionally) the ideas of social statics (those enduring elements of society that render stability and order) and social dynamics (those elements of society that impact change) (Turner, Beeghley, and Powers, 1989). This is one of the most fascinating facts of social life; that societies are both static and dynamic. That is, societies endure, are impermeable, and resist change ensuring their survival throughout time. On the other hand, societies are dynamic and mutable, as change is ever present. While this may be a secondary concern to many, it has been at the heart of much dialogue among sociologists.

This tension that exists in all societies between what we call immutability (order/stability) and mutability (change) is crucial to the student of the funerary. A casual observation of the funeral industry over the past 50 years reveals both elements of unchanging ritual and dramatic change. Why is understanding the cultural forces of change and stability important to the funeral service student? We will begin our quest to answer this question with a brief explanation of culture.

Culture

The word *culture* is used by many people in a diversity of contexts. However, sociologists use the term in a deliberate and precise manner. Ritzer (2013, p.116) describes culture as "...encompasses the ideas, values, practices and material objects that allow a group of people, even an entire society, to carry out their collective lives in relative order and harmony." Another definition, offered by Macionis (2008, p. 58), describes culture as "the ways of thinking, the ways of acting, and the material objects that together form a people's way of life. Culture includes what we think, how we act, and what we own. Culture is both our link to the past and our guide to the future."

There are many ways to understand the essence of culture. One helpful manner is to divide culture into material and non-material parts. Both definitions above include material and non-material elements of culture. In fact, Macionis (2008) and Ritzer (2013) address culture in this fashion in their introductory sociology textbooks. Material elements range from the clothes we wear to the various modes of transportation we use to the food we eat and the utensils employed to accomplish this activity. Non-material elements include values, ideas, concepts, and rules regarding acceptable and unacceptable behavior.

The funeral home director must be privy to both the material and non-material aspects of culture. For example, the instruments and chemicals used in body preparation for an open casket ceremony are all part of material culture. However, the ideas, values, and learned techniques in preparation of the body are part of the non-material culture. Upon closer examination, one can readily see a connection between the materials used and the ideas that guide their usage. Embalming fluids and the instruments used in cosmetic work are valued commodities for the funeral home director, family, friends, and the deceased. However, these cultural tools used for this type of body preparation do not make sense if the family has requested direct disposition. Burial and cremation, both socially legitimate forms of body disposition, are undergirded by non-material cultural elements of values, beliefs, and laws, as well as the policies of the funeral home and cemetery.

Another useful way to understand culture is dissect it into its constituent parts. At a minimum, the fundamental components of culture are values, symbols, and norms.

Components of Culture

Values. Benokratis (2014, p.44) defines values as "…standards by which members of a particular culture define what is good or bad, moral or immoral, proper or improper, desirable or undesirable, beautiful or ugly." Benokratis (2014) points out that values are shared by most and provide "general guidelines" for behavior rather than a set of rules for specific behavior. It is important to remember that values are widely shared but not "uniform." This is especially the case in more diverse and multicultural populations. It is this social space that gives rise to subculture, popular culture, high culture, and countercultures. These terms refer to segments of society that share some values with the larger community while holding other distinct values that set them apart.

One of the enduring values in American culture involves the recovery of bodies in human-made or natural disasters. Communities, as well as local, state, and federal agencies, will expend a great deal of funds to find and identify the remains of people. This particular "value" gives rise to policies and practices of agencies that are dedicated to this purpose.

Symbols. A symbol is anything that communicates or carries meaning among members of a culture. Clothes, hair style, facial and body expressions, cars, cell phones, mascots, icons, are just a few examples of *potential* symbols. Notice that we said "potential." In order for something to qualify as a symbol both parties must share in its meaning. Language is the most widely used symbol or set of symbols in a culture. In fact, some sociologists include language as a component of culture because of its dominant role in all cultures.

As stated, symbols carry meaning among members of a culture. Communication becomes precarious when symbols no longer share the same meaning. Imagine a situation in which one member of a culture provides a commentary of another person's athletic ability, and uses words such as "sick" or "bad" to describe his/her ability. If you did not know that these words could mean "exceptional" or perhaps more confusing, "good," you would conclude that the person was making a derogating comment. There are innumerable examples of how communication becomes fraught with problems when a symbol no longer is shared, or at best, is ambiguous.

For the funeral home director, attention to symbols is of critical importance. This includes understanding your client along a multitude of "symbol" rich variables such as age, religion, race/ethnicity, occupation, and socioeconomic class, just to name a few. Understanding symbols and effective communication is of the utmost importance in any client-professional relationship.

Norms. Norms are simply social rules. Norms are often divided into classes or categories, based on the significance of an act and depth of the reaction from others. "Folkways," as defined by Sumner (1940) are norms with little or no moral significance. This involves the majority of behavior viewed in everyday life, such as etiquette rules. For example, the appropriate use of utensils in a restaurant would likely fall within this category of norms. One would expect the use of a fork as opposed to fingers and hands while eating spaghetti. If you eat spaghetti with your fingers, you would certainly draw some frowns or negative reactions from other patrons, but there is little to no moral implication in such behavior.

Mores (pronounced- mawr-eyz), however, involves behavior that carries moral significance. Violation of this type of social rule often is accompanied by both informal (such as stigma, ostracism, etc.) and formal sanctions (fines, jail, or imprisonment). Many laws are included in this category of norms.

One important cautionary note is that the "act" should not be correlated with a particular category of norm without considering context and symbols. For example, the social reaction in our first example of eating spaghetti with fingers and hands in a restaurant depends entirely on context and symbols. An infant eating spaghetti with his/her hands in a baby chair and a bib will likely receive favorable comments from others and perhaps even elicit a few smiles and chuckles. It doesn't seem to invoke the same humor when it's a teenager in an act of defiance. While the "act" is the same, the interpretation of the two examples is much different.

For the funeral director, understanding social norms is imperative for effectively interacting with bereaved families. What makes this interaction more problematic is the cultural setting. In American culture, the social norms are not always clearly known or articulated. The grieving are often subject to ambiguity that places them at a disadvantage. Media, theatrical, and film perceptions of what grief "should look like" influence the behavior of the families we serve. As funeral service professionals, it is important to acknowledge the grief our clientele are experiencing and serve as a supportive resource. How many times do funeral directors quickly offer tissues when families begin to cry? Is this a passive way of asking the person to please stop crying and proceed with the arrangement? Sure, it is important to always have tissues ready for families, but does this message exist when a funeral director quickly pushes the box of tissues toward the crying family member? We need to remember that grief is a personal experience and acknowledge that it is real. It is incumbent upon the funeral director to understand how the family wishes to honor the deceased. Many critics have pointed to the excesses of the funeral home director by "overselling" products and services to his/her client. Understanding people through the lens of values, symbols, and norms can be advantageous to meeting the needs of the family and, simultaneously, muting critics. It is also valuable to acknowledge the reality that our society often teaches; in a polite society one does not discuss elements surrounding death. This no doubt causes the topic of death to be considered taboo in many corners of modern culture.

Building Blocks of Society

All societies provide structure for its members to engage in social life. These structures include roles, statuses, groups, organizations, and institutions. These five areas provide the context and opportunities for people to interact meaningfully with the larger community. Structures also signify a cultural identity. The building blocks of society may be viewed in hierarchal order, in which a lower level is subsumed within a higher level. The higher the level, the more abstract the building block is to an individual.

The most concrete building blocks (those closest to individuals) are statuses and roles. A status is a "socially recognized position that people occupy". Some of the most common statuses are occupational and familial statuses. A dentist, doctor, professor, manager, or funeral director are all examples of occupational statuses. Mother, father, brother, sister, cousin, etc. are all examples of familial statuses. Individuals occupy a multiplicity of statuses at any given time. Roles, on the other hand, are the expected behavior that are attached to one or more statuses. For example, a college student is a status (socially recognized position) and it is expected (roles) that this person buys books, attends classes, engages in homework and research, may join student clubs, etc.

A social group is defined as two or more people who engage in meaningful interaction. Different groups are defined by specific characteristics. For example, a primary group (Cooley, 1909), such as the family, is contrasted to a secondary group whose goal is to achieve some task, such as a work group. Organizations may be viewed as formal entities that are created to achieve some goal. Institutions are the most abstract of the building blocks and are defined by purpose and the function served in society.

Let us look at how this applies to the American funerary. As an institution, the American funerary serves two important functions (Kastenbaum, 2012). First, it provides a narrative or story about the loss of one of its members and the concomitant narratives of the survival of the community. The second function is the more practical matter of the disposal of the body. The totality of the American funerary fits into one of these two functions.

There are many organizations that comprise the institution of the funerary. For example, there are agencies or associations that monitor, set policy, or advocate for certain industry standards. Funeral homes, both corporate and privately owned, are also examples of organizations within the institution of the funerary. Other organizations would include the multifarious businesses that produce goods and services for funeral homes or cemeteries. The companies that make caskets, vaults, urns, or sell an assortment of services, including grief counseling, are all examples of organizations. Every organization is composed of social groups. The funeral home, for example, is a collection of one or more social groups. Depending upon the size of home, we might find several funeral directors, student apprentices, accounting and bookkeeping personnel, public relations staff, counselors, and people who provide services in the ceremony (ushers, information technology, etc.).

The institution of the funerary is full of statuses and roles. The bereaved is a status, as is the funeral home director, friends and extended family are also statuses (socially recognized position). Each of these has roles or socially expected behaviors. For example, the status of a "friend" is to console and provide support to the bereaved.

Social life seems to unfold in predictable patterns as long as all parties are playing their roles more or less within script. It is when people diverge from their script that social life becomes more ambiguous or simply in need of repair. Many funeral directors can share stories in which family (and sometimes friends) squabble over the possessions of the deceased or if there is stark disagreement on how to conduct the funeral rite, or the estranged son who takes all by surprise and gracefully acknowledges his fathers' life and death and serves as a unifying force during the arrangement process. The unpredictable nature surrounding emotions and behaviors when death is encountered challenges expected statuses and roles. For the funeral director, understanding the building blocks of society, especially statuses and roles, can be crucial in managing conflict or disagreement among family, friends, colleagues, or work groups.

Socialization

One of the most profound questions that sociologists have addressed over the years is how does an individual become a member of a culture? Or how does culture get inside of the individual? Sociologists have referred to this process as socialization or enculturation. While a full treatment of the subject would require many volumes of work, there are a few concepts that will aid the student of the funerary. The following ideas are central concepts of socialization:

1)   <u>Socialization is an ongoing process, from birth to death.</u>
        While it may be correct that much of one's personality is
        forged during the early years in one's life, the
        socialization process is ongoing and enduring. In part,
        this hinges on the dynamism of culture and new
        experiences one faces throughout life. We are forever
        negotiating and renegotiating cultural norms, values, and
        symbols. In this sense, we are part of a dialectic process,
        in which we impact culture and in turn, culture imprints
        itself on us.

2)   <u>Socialization is both formal and informal.</u> By formal, we
        mean those times and places that are intentionally carved
        out to learn culture. School, for example, is one setting
        in which socialization is formal. You learn about your
        world and culture in classes that teach language,
        mathematics, history, geography, etc. However, much of
        our socialization occurs in informal venues or spaces. It
        is what we learn about culture during informal
        socialization that is often connected to "how the world
        really works." Have you ever been trained for a job in
        which you were given the step-by-step book
        instructions? Then you notice after a few weeks that very
        few people, who are doing the same job, are in full
        compliance to the book. In fact, you notice that it is
        difficult to stay on task if you adhere to the instructions
        out of the book. Your observation of fellow employees is
        an example of informal socialization. Of course, the
        degree of acceptable deviation from a work manual
        varies according to occupation.

3) Socialization is never perfect. The process of learning
    one's culture through the socialization process is always
    imperfect and incomplete. The social-psychological
    theoretical perspectives are beyond the scope of this text.
    Human behavior does not neatly fit into an automaton
    model in which one generation is perfectly and
    completely socialized from the previous generation.
    Socialization is connected to interpretation, negotiation,
    and definitions of the situations. This provides a great
    deal of variation in how someone might act and define
    his/her act in a given context.

The socialization or enculturation process has been a topic of
extensive research by sociologists and psychologists alike. While
a plethora of perspectives and theories exist, the three concepts
described above have widespread support. We now turn our
attention to the final section of this chapter, and examine a few
ideas regarding social rituals.

The Role of Rituals in Social Life

Social rituals are habituated patterns of activity that carry
significant meaning. Often, we use the term "ritual" in the
broadest sense that describes daily habits. The common use of
this term creates confusion for many students when learning
about the importance of the social ritual. For example, on days
off from work, one might have the ritual of drinking coffee and
reading theory books at a local coffee shop. It is certainly
ritualistic in terms of a "habit" or habituated pattern of activity.
In addition, the habit may even have "meaning" to someone.
However, it does not carry the same significance as a funeral

service, graduation ceremony, public elections, confirmation, baptism, or a myriad of social and religious activities.

Social rituals, among other things, must include both habituated patterns of activity and be imbued with meaning that exceeds everyday life activities (such as visiting coffee shops, lunch destinations, dinner at a specific restaurant on a specific evening of the week, etc.). Clearly, the end-of-life activities by family and friends of the deceased may be viewed in the broadest sense as a social ritual. Wakes, funeral services (regardless of the name - memorial service, funeral service, or celebration of life, etc.), vigils, and body preparation/disposition are all parts of ritual.

The importance of funerary rituals cannot be understated. They provide survivors and the community with important moments for reflection, closure, grief work, memorializing the deceased, and assurance that the community will survive beyond the loss of one member.

Given the gravity of the funerary as social ritual, it is imperative for the funeral director to provide a context of meaning for the surviving family and friends. While the sanctity and solemnity of the funerary rituals are still intact, the expression, symbols, norms, and meaning are mutable (subject to change). The modern funeral director is challenged by a rapidly changing set of values, attitudes, symbols, and norms related to funerary rituals by the presence of a global and diverse clientele. We argue that the institution of the funerary, along with the status and roles of the funeral director, has changed dramatically over the past 40-50 years. A sociological perspective will equip the funeral director with the requisite conceptual tools to understand the changes in both ritual and roles, as well as the underlying context of such changes.

Important Foundations of Sociology to Consider

- **Ceremony (Ritual):** An action conducted during a rite which may or may not have symbolic meaning to the participants or witnesses of the rite.

- **Culture Shock:** The feelings of disorientation, uncertainty, and even fear experienced when one encounters an unfamiliar cultural practice.

- **Cultural Relativism:** The viewing of people's behavior from the perspective of one's own culture.

- **Cultural Universal:** A common practice or belief shared by all societies.

- **Diffusion:** The process by which a cultural item spreads from group to group or society to society.

- **Ethnocentrism:** The propensity to believe that one's own culture and way of life represent what's normal or are superior to all others.

- **Innovation:** The process of introducing a new idea or object to a culture through discovery or invention.

- **Religion:** A culturally embedded configuration of behavior made up of sacred beliefs, emotional feelings accompanying the beliefs, and overt behavior seemingly executing the beliefs and feelings.

- **Religious Ritual:** A practice required or expected of members of a faith.

- **Social Function:** An event that allows people to share something of which they have in common.

- **Sociobiology:** The systematic study of how biology affects human social behavior.

- **Symbol:** A gesture, object, or word that forms the basis of human communication.

Chapter 1

Student Discussion Points

- How would you define sociology?
- Why is it important for funeral service professionals to study sociology?
- What has been the impact of globalization on society and specifically on the funeral service industry?
- What did Comte mean when he indicated societies are both static and dynamic?
- Explain the components of culture.
- Explain the structures necessary for members of society to engage in social life.
- What is socialization, and how does it work?
- Explain the role of rituals in social life?

Chapter Two: Societal Changes that Impact Funeral Service

Chapter Editor: Joseph R. Finocchiaro, CFSP

Chapter 2 Learning Objectives

- Discuss Industrialization and its impact on the funeral service industry.
- Explain the Post-Industrialization adaptive strategy.
- Describe Urbanization and its impact on the funeral service industry.
- Deliberate the impact of Bureaucracies and Institutions.
- Elaborate on the reality of greater life expectancy.

~ SOCIETAL CHANGES THAT IMPACT FUNERAL SERVICE ~

The practice of honoring our dead through rites and pageantry are considered among the oldest of social traditions. Contemporary funeral practices are rooted in tradition and shaped by the past, but they also reflect change that uniquely underscores current attitudes, values, and norms. As implied in the preceding chapter, funeral professionals must be able to adapt to temporary fluctuations as well as more permanent changes. The funeral professional is both a guardian of the past and a harbinger of the future. Practitioners must be privy to the past and sensitive to the emergent trends within the context of a multicultural society.

As stated in Chapter One, social life is subject to change. This is one of the enduring realities of human existence. Of course, some of these changes are minor and nearly insignificant, for example fads or current fashion. There are other types of changes that have a much broader impact on people that shape the course of their lives through the socialization process. These types of changes are paradigm shifts, which have a broad and deep impact on how societies are organized.

Many of these changes have been prompted by new technologies. We often equate technology with computers or computer-related things. Indeed, computers are a big part of our modern technology. Technology, in the broader sense, includes material culture, tools, or ideas that people use to manage everyday existence. Consider the following: a stick, a shovel, and a tractor. Each of these embodies in some fashion a technology. In a few simple economies, a digging stick is the technology used to help plant food. In other communities, a shovel may be the extent of the technology for food production. In more modern communities, a tractor is commonplace. Each of these technologies impact individuals and communities in terms of organization. It may only take 25 workers with shovels to do the same quantity of work as 100 people with digging sticks, and perhaps one person on a tractor could do all the work of 125 workers with shovels and digging sticks within the first hour of the work day. In all three, cases we might ask the questions "What skills are most valued?" or "What percentage of the community must be dedicated to food production to ensure the survival of its people?" Technologies help shape the adaptive strategies (economy) and, ultimately, the manner in which societies are organized.

As a final example, consider the technological marvel of the combustible engine. Fossil fuel engines proved to be more efficient and consistent than the earlier steam engine. With the advent of efficient engines, the further invention and development of the automobile has had a far-reaching impact on social life. People could live in one area and work many miles away. Improved transportation, in terms of speed, distance, and dependability, provided the underpinnings that would lead to new patterns of living, including the development of suburbs. This has helped to define a broad swath of American life for much of the twentieth century. How much of your time is devoted to commuting from one place to another? The technology and use of the automobile also brought us traffic jams, pollution, tag fees, drivers licenses, auto insurance, and highway fatalities, just to name a few.

Not only have these technologies significantly impacted social life, but they have also made their mark on the funeral service industry. In this chapter, we introduce a few of the broad reaching structural changes to society and social life over the past few hundred years, including: industrialization, post-industrialization, urbanization, bureaucratization and social institutions, and greater life expectancy. While these changes are interrelated, each merits individual attention.

Industrialization

Industrialization is the process by which a society transforms from a primarily agricultural adaptive strategy (economy) to the manufacturing of goods and services through advanced technical enterprises. The Industrial Revolution took place during the 18th and 19th centuries. Prior to this time, societies in Europe and colonial America were primarily agrarian and rural. The production of goods was accomplished by craftsman, most often in people's homes or on farms, using hand tools and basic machines. Industrialization manifested a shift to powered, specialized machinery, factories and mass production. As this new form of the production of goods enveloped society, the need for the skills that were vital in the previous era declined. Families, once noted for their craftsmanship, were displaced in the economic structure by the prominence of the factory of the Industrial Revolution.

The advent of industrialism, with new technologies in design, machines, and power, changed the manner in which work was accomplished. While much of the attention has been directed toward new ways of harnessing energy and the inventions themselves, what is most often overlooked are the dramatic changes to social life that such discoveries cause.

Division of labor. One of the consequences of industrialization is a more complex division of labor in the manner in which goods are produced. In agrarian and rural societies, the division of labor tends to be more simplex. For example, if you owned a funeral home in pre-industrial times, you might have an assistant to help you, but you, yourself, would likely play a heavy role in preparing the body for burial, building the casket, digging the hole for interment, conducting the service, and maybe singing the selection of songs. In other words, the division of labor is simplex. In today's parlance, you would be the "jack of trades."

Contrast this to the industrial and post-industrial societies, in which the division of labor (the production of goods and services) is complex and multi-layered. It is characterized by "specialization". Today's funeral homes, for example, are highly specialized. Consider the following career tracks within the funeral industry: funeral directors, embalmers, managers, pre-need specialists, receptionists, accountants, crematory operators, and grief counselors. Companies external to your funeral home provide vaults, caskets, urns, jewelry, and an assortment of other goods and services. What about cemetery space, and other funeral related services? In other words, it is highly improbable that you would do more than one or two of these roles in today's society. Industrial societies, therefore, are characterized by a complex division of labor and highly specialized roles (Durkheim, 1964).

Growth of Middle Class. Another impact of industrialization is the growth of a middle class. As goods and services became more plentiful and less expensive in mass production, more people are able to afford more goods and services. It is also important to note that the growth of the middle class is associated with other social variables such as politics, values, social movements, etc. The work of labor unions, for example, pressed for higher wages and better work conditions (Schlesinger, 2011). This provided greater leverage for families to afford factory-built automobiles, televisions, and home appliances.

Leisure. As a society moves from an agrarian based economy, characterized by the use of animal-powered plows to an agricultural based economy, characterized by machines powered by fossil fuels, less time is devoted to farming and gathering food for a community. This is clearly seen in employment trends over the past 100 years. In 1900, more than 40% of our population was dedicated to food production. Today, less than two percent of the population is dedicated to food production. The use of machinery powered by fossil fuels and new designs in the how human capital is used provides more time for leisure.

Post-Industrialization

Post-Industrialization is a type of adaptive strategy (economy) that is based on high-technologies (computers) and information rather than the production of goods. While manufacturing may still be present, a greater percentage of the economy is connected to high-technologies, information, and complex systems of communication.

Countries dominated by a post-industrial economy are also characterized by the exportation of information, knowledge, and high-tech goods. Conversely, many of these same countries import manufactured goods. The textile industry, for example, has been largely non-existent in the United States for decades. Most of these products are imported from China, Mexico, Korea, India, etc. Production costs, including wages, tend to be lower in these countries. These areas can simply produce consumable products at a price point that is difficult for post-industrial economies to match. There is always a degree of tension in these two competing realities of post-industrial, or information-based economies, and industrial, or manufacturing based economies. In the U.S., for example, it may feel patriotic to buy products made in America, but there is a competing narrative with purchasing the same product at a lower cost made elsewhere. The interplay between these two narratives makes for interesting politics and marketing strategies.

Urbanization

Urbanization involves living patterns that reflect a high density of people in a relatively bounded space. In the United States, for example, 1920 marks the year when more people lived in urban than rural areas. This shift in living patterns, from rural to urban areas, has been fueled by industrialization. The transition to an urban society has a far reaching impact on the social life and social relations. For the funeral professional, this shift cannot be underestimated. In the United States, cities evolved and became the hub of economic and cultural activity in the late 19th century that would shape much of cultural life throughout the 20th century.

One of the most profound changes (as it relates to the funeral professional) in urban life involves social relationships. Sociologists have documented the dramatic as well as the subtle changes in social relationships between urban, rural, and kinship life. One of the notable changes involves the nature of social roles. There are at least three points that are cogent to this discussion. First, the sheer number of roles that one is expected to play expands within the urban context. This drives the nature of social interaction toward more "impersonal interaction". Second, these roles tend to be more specialized, segmented, and rational. In other words, your interaction with people is not with the whole or entirety of the individual, but rather a sliver of a person operating within a finite role. Finally, the role playing tends to be prompted by self-interest rather than the interest of the kinship (Tonnies, 1963).

Consider a few of your activities and corresponding roles in terms of these three points. On your way to work you stop by a coffee shop and order food and a latte. Your interaction with the barista is typically confined to your food and beverage order, and of course, payment for the products. Unless you are a close friend or relative, you will likely engage in small talk about the weather, upcoming holidays, or the score of last night's college basketball game. Leaving the coffee shop, you realize that you need to sign those forms at your bank. You rush into the lobby to speak to a teller. As you sign the papers, you share your thoughts on the upcoming football game and again, the weather. You finally make it to work. You are a nurse at a local allergy clinic. You consider your work rewarding, as you help people cope with their allergies, but your day is chock-full of superficial conversations with a wide variety of people from different backgrounds. You discuss the scores of college or professional sports teams, new movies, the latest hit TV series, and again, the weather. On your way home, you stop by the cleaners to pick up your clothes and again, you find yourself discussing the weather or some other superficial theme. Urban life (including suburban life) is marked by interactions with different others in highly specialized, segmented, and rational contexts. All of these examples underscore the nature of the roles within the urban life. There are few, if any, deep, personal, and gratifying social exchanges.

Another facet of urban existence is the high degree of social anonymity. By social anonymity, we mean that people are relatively unknown to the larger community. In a sense, one's identity is relegated to a plethora of impersonal roles that are played throughout the day, none of which impact the larger community in any significant manner. This is what makes death in modernity so difficult. Other than a few friends and immediate family, the death of any individual has little, if any, impact on the larger community. The funeral professional must be cognizant of this reality. We are convinced that a more personalized, individualized ritual for the deceased will continue to supplant the more generic type. The personalized funerary experience is the last attempt on the part of the decedent to decry the anonymity of urban living (more on this in Chapter 5- Trends).

Bureaucracies and Institutions

Another feature of the modern world is the prominence of bureaucracy and institutions. For the purpose of this book, we couple these two realities, although a separate book could be written on each of these topics. Max Weber (1978) was one of the first scholars (and sociologists) to write about the growth of bureaucracies and detail its social arrangements. Bureaucracy is a method of administrative system governing any large institution, be it public or private. Bureaucratic institutions are enduring and impersonal in asserting and sustaining power.

The advent of the bureaucratic organization has completely enveloped social life to the extent that we hardly recognize or understand its impact. Bureaucracy is ubiquitous and the hallmark achievement of the modern world. There are few goods or services that we consume each day that are not somehow touched by the bureaucratic organization, whether it's the food we eat or the entertainment that we watch.

The impact of the bureaucratic model has significantly impacted the funeral service industry, both in the complexities of caring for the dead and their surviving family. It became the work of the funeral director to secure items such as death certificates, burial transit permits, and other legal documents. Funeral homes must also remain within compliance of the Environmental Protection Agency (EPA), Occupational Safety and Health Administration (OSHA), Federal Trade Commission (FTC), and the Americans with Disabilities Act (ADA) to name but a few governing bodies or laws. The life of the rural town funeral director serving a small community is an artifact of the past. The complexity of the funeral industry is embedded in the context of a bureaucratic-dominated society.

Institutions are another social organizing feature of the modern world. By institution, we mean relatively large, formal secondary groups. These institutions are guided by a bureaucratic organizational model. We address the expansion of institutions as a feature of modernity to underscore the broad transition and differences between kinship and agrarian life to an urban orientation. The twentieth century was marked by the expansion of massive institutions within nearly every sector of social institutions, including banking, health care, transportation, criminal justice, education, and likely your career, just to name a few. Technically, these organizations should not be confused with the social institutions as described in chapter one.

Much of our existence is lived within the boundaries of these massive social institutions. Consider the number of life hours that have been spent within the boundaries of education. It's not just the time devoted to the classroom from kindergarten (or pre-K) to 12th grade, but all of the related time dedicated to study, orientations, parent-teacher conferences, co-curricular and extra-curricular activities. Of course, your interaction with these large social institutions may not conclude with a high school diploma. Your pursuit of a college degree will compel you to invest more of your time with this institution.

It is important for the funeral professional to understand the role of institutions and large bureaucratic organizations in social life. Hospitals, retirement communities, and nursing homes are a few examples of institutional life. These are the places where people die. Improved medical practices and advanced medical technologies means that the dying processes for many have been delayed into their elderly years. It is common for people to die in institutions as opposed to in their own homes. As a result, death has become less visible to modern America.

A brief view of statistics on this matter supports our claim. In 1900, as many as 80% of all people in the U.S. died in their own homes. Today, approximately 68% of those who die in the U.S. do so within the boundaries of an institution (Corr & Corr, 2013). The twentieth century is characterized by the pervasiveness and intrusion of large bureaucratic institutions into our private lives. People more often than not die within these institutions and, in a sense, removed from the view of family and friends. The dying is done out of sight of friends, family, and in the larger sense, even society. The sanitation of end of life issues logically leads to the sanitation of funeral services. The funeral service practitioner has experienced less demand for embalming and services with the body present and more focus on celebrations of life with no body present. Even more disconcerting is the trend toward direct disposition where there is absolutely no remembrance of the decedent through rite or memorialization.

Greater Life Expectancy

Greater life expectancy is a correlate of modernity. Improvements in technology, medicine, and public administration (especially regulations regarding water and food) over the past century continues to push life expectancy to new heights. During the twentieth century, overall average life expectancy in the United States increased from fewer than 50 years to 76.7 years (Corr & Corr, 2013, pg. 27). The Centers for Disease Control (CDC) estimated the 2011 U. S. life expectancy at 78.7 years (76.3 for males; 81.1 years for females). When compared to 1940 life expectancy of 62.9 (60.8 for males; 65.2 for females), the evidence is clear; Americans are living longer (CDC, n.d.). Advancements in health care and pharmaceuticals, new tools for disease prevention and diagnosis, and increased safety awareness (mandatory seatbelt use, less environmental pollution, greater workplace safety, etc.) have all served to extend our lives into old age.

The U.S. population of 65 years of age and over is expected to reach 72 million people by the year 2030 (ICAA, 2009). The age group 85 and older is now the fastest growing segment of the population. As we age, our circle of friends and family may diminish, as well as our financial resources. Others may be left with the monetary burden when faced with final arrangements. The fear of rising funeral costs along with geographic distance from one's hometown may influence people to utilize the affordability and portability of cremation (Fritch & Altieri, 2015).

The realities of longer life and rising costs are added pressures to growing old. What are the implications for the funeral service professional? It is not unusual for people to outlive their retirement plans and savings that they were able to secure during their working years, leaving little to address funeral arrangements. This may lead people to select less expensive merchandise and disposition options that directly impact funeral home business plans. It is also the case that, as people age, they consider and complete their own arrangements, which often includes the selection of minimal services and merchandise. In addition, family members have more time to say good bye to loved ones who live into their elderly years. This opportunity to honor them while alive obviates, for some, the need to honor them with elaborate funerary expenses. Although increasing life expectancies underscores an important value in American culture, it comes with additional challenges for the general public and the funeral service industry.

Now that we have provided you with a few sociological tools (Chapter One) and discussed briefly a few historic trends that have shaped modernity and as a result, bounded the funeral industry within a particular context or framework, we are ready to explore a litany of variables that directly bear on the funeral industry.

Chapter 2

Student Discussion Points

- Explain and discuss Industrialization and how this process has impacted funeral service.
- How have changes in the division of labor affected funeral service?
- Explain and discuss Post-Industrialization and associated impacts on funeral service. How has this changed our economy?
- Explore the reality of Urbanization.
- What are Bureaucracies and how do they impact funeral service?
- How would you define Institutions from a sociological perspective, and how is this related to funeral service.
- Discuss the impact of greater life expectancy on society, and specifically, on the funeral service industry.

Chapter Three: The Sociology of Funeral Service

Chapter Editor: Doug Ferrin, M.S.

Chapter 3 Learning Objectives

- Examine the difference between funeral and memorial services as well as funeral rites.
- Learn the central connection between sociology and funeral service.
- Explore various family governance systems.
- Study various family structures.
- Consider various human relationships and living arrangements.

~ THE SOCIOLOGY OF FUNERAL SERVICE ~

The human experience without death is incomplete, yes; the final act for all human beings is death. The implications of this reality, the uncertainty associated with the death process and what happens after death, compels funeral service professionals to study sociology. Death and related rituals are "social" to the core. This is the basis for funeral service professionals to be grounded in the scientific discipline of sociology.

The practice of honoring our dead, and the associated rites and pageantry, are considered to be among the oldest of social traditions. Contemporary funeral practices are both a collection of traditions and a bundle of changes. As noted in the preceding chapters, funeral professionals must be nimble and inclined to adapt to changing environments. It is important for the funeral profession to remember that both funeral and memorial services are social functions and funerary rituals (although they vary) are considered to be culturally universal.

Funerals, Memorial Services, and Funeral Rites

At the onset of this section, it is important to define a few of the terms used in this section for clarification. First, a funeral rite is considered to be an all-inclusive term referring to all funerals and memorial services, while a funeral service is defined as rites with the physical body present, and a memorial service is an event in which the body is not present. This raises a fundamental question; "what is a funeral rite and why do people attend?"

The Purpose for Sociology in Funeral Service

The central connection between funeral service and sociology is dichotomous in nature; a funeral rite is both a social function and a cultural universal. First and foremost, a funeral rite is a social function – an event that allows people to share something of which they have in common. In the instance of funerals, the cohesion element is the deceased. People who participate in the funeral rite are not required to actually have known the deceased; indeed, they may be friends with members of the deceased's family. They may feel compelled to participate by proxy, or at minimum acknowledge the loss and reassure the family of their support. It has been said that death can bring out the best, or the worst, in people. Regardless of individual grieving strategies, death will draw a group of people together. We do not mean that this is intended to unify family and friends, it is simply acknowledging that a death is a focal point, an event allowing people to share an experience they have in common.

The second critical element of funeral service as it is related to sociology is the realization that a funeral rite is cultural universal - a common practice or belief shared by all societies. As designated earlier in this chapter, funeral rites are considered to be one of the oldest social traditions in the world. Although funeral rites and traditions are both diverse and unique in many ways, the reality is that all societies throughout history have in some fashion performed funeral rites. The exact rites conducted are typically unique and are impacted by cultural, geographical, religious, ethnic, and other elements specific to the deceased. Regardless of the various elements that help determine the funeral rites, all will typically have specific guidelines with respect to the announcement of the death, prescriptions related to the human remains, appropriate method(s) for disposition of the remains, and guidelines on celebration of life through ceremony, ritual, or memorialization. Have you personally experienced or witnessed different approaches to these components of funeral rites? How would you describe these events and what do you believe was the driving force behind what you witnessed?

It is an honor each time a funeral director has the opportunity to work with a grieving family, and in some way, manages to reduce the burden of the experience on the family – no doubt this is a rewarding experience. An essential component of the successful arrangement conference is building a trusted relationship with the family. Trust is earned. Part of earning trust is to establish rapport with the family during the grieving process.

In the next few pages, we will briefly describe the importance of the role of the family, both in terms of governance and structure, and the myriad of ways that people organize themselves into a family unit. A working knowledge of both family governance systems and common family structures assist funeral professionals as they work to better understand our diverse culture.

Family Governance Systems

In order to understand family governance systems it is first necessary to define family. Witt (2011) provides a substantive definition of the family, a definition of the family based on blood, meaning shared genetic heritage, and law, meaning social recognition and affirmation of the bond including both marriage and adoption.

In addition to a substantive perspective, it is valuable to consider a functionalist definition. Sociologist William F. Ogburn identified six primary functions that families perform, these include: reproduction, socialization, protection, regulation of sexual behavior, affection and companionship, and provision of social status (Witt, 2011). For the purpose of this text we have elected to present three common family governance systems: patriarchal, matriarchal, and egalitarian.

When working with a family, you will witness different decision making styles. Sometimes arrangement decisions must be approved by either the man, woman, or they may truly be joint decisions. You will also experience families who are unable to make decisions. This is especially the case when the deceased played the primary role as the decision-maker. It is not uncommon during these arrangements to overhear family members asking questions such as, "what would mom have wanted?" or "what would dad have done?" In each case, you can learn about family governance systems by carefully listening.

Patriarchal governance is a situation in which males dominate or are the primary decision-makers. Conversely, matriarchal governance locates the decision-making to the females. Egalitarian governance is a model in which spouses are regarded as equals. Garnering this type of knowledge about families can help funeral directors better understand their clients and be able to better serve their individual needs.

Family Structures

Historically, the family has served as the primary resource for our needs, both physical and emotional. Members of a family grow to count on other family members for various essentials including food, shelter, and knowledge. Most people grow up with a belief that their own family experience is similar to everyone else's. This assumption is not founded in research. We have briefly considered the difference between a substantive approach and a functional approach in understanding the core components of a family. Furthermore, we identified three specific family governance systems in hopes to better understand the different family experiences that exist in our culture. Professional Training Schools (2012) indicate there are as many as 20-25 identifiable types of family systems; here we explore a few of the most common in our society. It is important to note that in our ever-changing society, families are also subject to change. The functions, expectations, and even the structures will change over time. It is our goal at this point to introduce family structures commonly encountered by funeral service professionals in contemporary society.

Many consider the most common family in our society today is the nuclear family, a structure consisting of a married couple and their unmarried children living together. Married couples with children under 18 make up 32 percent of total families (Witt, 2011). This is not to be confused with the family model idealized in the 1950s with the father as the breadwinner, and the homebound mom. According to the Bureau of Labor Statistics (2009), this only makes up 9.8 percent of total families and only 21 percent of families with children under 18 years of age. In fact, the percentage of single-parent and non-family households has risen steadily over the past 50 years (Witt, 2011).

The next family structure to consider is the extended family. An extended (joint) family is one in which relatives, such as grandparents, aunts, or uncles live in the same household as parents and their children. Although this family structure is not as common today, without question, this living arrangement is still seen today among segments of the population. As the middle class grew in number and wealth, the extended family faded into the background. However, life events such as death, divorce, illness or unemployment often necessitate the extended family structure. This can provide additional physical, emotional, and financial support. We also find extended families who are affiliated in a common business venture or adherence to a strict religious doctrine.

Another structure that developed to combat the daily struggle of life is a hybrid version of the extended family structure, known as the modified extended family. This is a household or family fashioned by related nuclear families and/or friendships, with the purpose to provide added support and resources for the entire group. Although the modified extended family is most likely composed of related nuclear families or friendships, it is possible for church groups, neighbors, and work colleagues to initiate and participate in this modified family structure.

Other family structures include the single parent family and the blended family. A blended family is identified as a family unit consisting of one male and one female, their children together, and any children they each may have from previous marriages or relationships. According to Witt (2011, pg 166), 15 percent of children under 18 years of age live in a step-family structure. This, of course, is the result of single parents who marry or divorced parents who remarry.

Other arrangements include: 1) those who elect to remain single; 2) those who choose to cohabitate but never marry; 3) those who marry but choose not to have children; 4) those who choose a same-sex marriage. This final family structure is the result of a recent U.S. Supreme Court ruling that grants same-sex marriage as a right. As we view the dynamic nature of social life, it is important to remain mindful of the changing family structures in our society. The more insight we have of our own society, the better equipped we will be to serve the families that enter our funeral homes

Relationships and Living Arrangements

Our final section in this chapter involves relationships and living arrangements. An understanding of these crucial components will aid us in evaluating the impact on funeral service and funeral rites. These relationships and arrangements undeniably guide the decisions families make regarding funeral arrangements and the funeral rites. In this final section, we consider the issues of divorce, same-sex relationships, cohabitants, and those who decide to live as single adults.

Although divorce statistics can be difficult to interpret (Witt, 2011), the fact is that many marriages end in divorce. It is routine for media outlets to report that approximately one out of every two marriages ends in divorce. It is also estimated that 63 percent of all divorced people in the United States have remarried. What are the sociological impacts of divorce regarding funeral service? Divorce may give rise to challenges if there is considerable disagreement with current and prior marital relationships. These concerns are even more multifaceted when children are involved or if a former spouse remarries. When the need arises for divorced families to make funeral arrangements, the funeral rites desired can differ among members of the family.

In addition, the parties that claim to be the legal next-of-kin can be numerous. It is therefore important that funeral service professionals work diligently to determine the authentic authorized agent(s). In addition, funeral directors will face the continual challenge of meeting the expectations of a myriad of family members, while following the directives of the authorizing agent. It is reasonable to believe that the occurrence of divorce will continue to be commonplace. Most states have adopted less restrictive divorce laws. This trend, coupled with more professional opportunities for women than in the past, creates a greater context for financial independence. Funeral service providers will be expected to manage and navigate this reality.

Another social factor to consider is same-sex partnerships, lesbian and gay relationships, and same-sex marriage. As previously stated, the U.S. Supreme Court ruled that same-sex marriage is a nationwide right (2015). This ruling formalizes what has been an increasing trend in U.S. culture. The United State Census Bureau estimated that approximately 594,000 same-sex couple households lived in the United States in 2010. Some challenges of contemporary funeral directors when working with same-sex couples were addressed with the Supreme Court ruling. For example, many funeral professionals recall working with a family in which the deceased's surviving significant other was not able to make arrangements. They were subject to the wishes of the biological family to include them in the arrangement process. Funeral service professionals must understand that the same factors of faith, culture, tradition, and family preference will drive funeral rite decisions for all groups of people, including same-sex couples. The goal of all activities of the professional funeral director is to help grieving families through the funerary rituals.

Cohabitation, two unrelated adults living together, is another living arrangement. Approximately 50 percent of the married couples in the United States report that they lived together prior to marriage. In the U.S. today, more than eight percent of opposite-sex couples are unmarried. Cohabitation is more common among African Americans and American Indians than among other racial and ethnic groups, and it is least common among Asian Americans (Witt, 2011). It is also notable that while cohabitation is associated with younger couples, it is a growing phenomenon among working adults. It is believed that about half of the people involved in cohabitation were previously married.

Cohabitation is functioning as a transitory or permanent alternative to marriage for many men and women who have experienced their own or their parents' divorce. Cohabitation may provide additional challenges for funeral home directors. The funeral rites that a person desires may not be congruent with family expectations. It is incumbent on the funeral service professional to offer all options, work to serve the family in a dignified manner, and determine the legal authorized agent, and follow their requests. Much like many of the other living arrangements and family relationships mentioned in this book, many of the challenges presented to funeral directors rest with determining the party with legal disposition rights, and working to minimize the pain associated with the funeral process. Funeral directors must be mindful that social change also includes the type of merchandise, services, and rites that are fashionable at a given point in time.

It is also useful to mention that many adults choose to remain single. For many reasons people may decide that a single life is best for lifestyle. Regardless of the motivation, one challenge to the funeral professional is the determination of who will serve as the legal next-of-kin/authorized agent when the time comes to make funeral arrangements. If a single person, with no children, does not assign someone as their authorized agent, it is possible that in death, no one will be around to see that final arrangements will be made. This cohort may have vastly different preferences than their family history.

Funeral professionals, like all people, come from varying backgrounds and family structures. Coming from a particular structure or background may lead a person to believe his or her family structure is superior to others. It is important to remember that the funeral director's professionalism isn't enhanced by judging the culture, religion, or social structure of the deceased or the bereaved.

Chapter 3

Student Discussion Points

- Explain the difference between a funeral service, memorial service, and a funeral rite.
- Why study the relationship between sociology and funeral service?
- What is meant by the term "Cultural Universal" and how is it related to the funeral service industry?
- Name and discuss various family governance systems.
- Explain various family structures.
- Discuss various social relationships and living arrangements, and how these impact the funeral service industry.

Chapter Four: Social Factors that Impact Funeral Rites

Chapter Editor: David S. Hess, M.S. Ed.

Chapter Learning Objectives

- Explore the impacts of economics and government on society and funeral service.
- Examine demographics, what they are, and how they can be utilized in society and in the funeral service industry.
- Define and explore social stratification.
- Acknowledge and explain the impact of religion on society, and the funeral service industry.
- Examine the impact of geographic factors on the funeral service industry.

~ SOCIAL FACTORS THAT IMPACT FUNERAL RITES ~

Despite the unique nature of the funeral service profession, and specifically funeral rites, ultimately, many of the same social factors that impact other industries and social institutions also influence funeral rites and the industry as a whole. These items include the impact of government, economics and religion, as well as conditions surrounding individual's ethnic background and specific circumstances regarding relationships and living arrangements. Here, you will read about several social factors that have direct implications on the funeral service profession and, specifically, on funeral rites.

Economics & Government

Economics is the study of how resources are allocated among alternative uses to satisfy human wants (Mansfield & Behravesh, 1998). As previously stated, its impact on society, governmental policies, strategies, and the funeral service profession and funeral rites is significant. A fundamental principle of economics is supply and demand. This simply means that the business sector will supply the demands of the public market. The impact on the funeral service industry merits discussion in this section. For example, the increasing demand for cremation has prompted directors of funeral homes and cemeteries to adjust their business practices to accommodate the growing demand.

In addition, the cyclical nature of a nation's economy directly affects the goods, services, and funeral rites people choose when making funeral arrangements. During recessions, people generally spend less on goods and services. This applies to goods and services offered by funeral homes. As a funeral service practitioner, it is important to be privy to these fluctuations in the overall health of the economy.

Although overall spending on arrangements will likely decrease during recessions, it is also true that funeral arrangements have an inelastic demand (few close substitutes). This means that client families will still arrange for funeral services but will likely make choices that are less expensive. Conversely, when an economy is experiencing periods of economic growth, all else being equal, people generally elect to spend more when making funeral arrangements. This translates to more expenditures on goods and services offered by funeral homes. Ultimately, the state of the economy influences client expenditures of funeral service goods and services.

We must note that there is a presumed correlation between the labor pool and economy. During struggling economies, there is an increase in individuals expressing interest in entering the industry. During recessions, people lose jobs and are searching for a career that is somewhat stable (inelasticity). This does provide some employment stability. Conversely, during times of economic growth, there is a general reduction in the overall interest in the funeral service industry.

Various economic systems exist, and they are typically directly related to the prevailing government type. A few major economic systems include capitalism (based on private property, in which profit-seeking individuals, companies, and corporations compete in the marketplace), socialism (the means of production and distribution are collectively owned), and what is known as a mixed economy, which is a system that combines elements of both capitalism and socialism. The type of economic system will dictate many elements related to how a funeral service business operates. Is the business for profit and owned by a sole proprietor, partnership or corporation, or is the industry operated by the state/government with little personal incentive to excel?

The type of government in which a business operates is also a significant factor. Types of governments include: 1) monarchy (headed by a single member of a royal family), 2) oligarchy (a few individuals rule), 3) dictatorship (one person has nearly total power to make and enforce laws), 4) totalitarianism (virtually complete government control and surveillance over all aspects of a society's social and political life), and 5) democracy (government by the people). Although these are considered the five major types of governments, in most cases, actual types of governance are hybrid versions of these major categories. For example, the United States is often considered to be a representative democracy, meaning that members of Congress, and state legislatures, elected by the people, make the laws that govern society.

The type of government, and the regulations that govern business practices, will determine the boundaries of business operations. For example, in the U.S., the Federal Trade Commission (FTC), Environmental Protection Agency (EPA), Occupational Safety and Health Administration (OSHA), and the Internal Revenue Service (IRS), all play a role in how funeral service practitioners operate their respective businesses. Regulation, for example, typically increases the cost of doing business for funeral homes. These costs are passed on to the consumer. There is inherent tension between regulations and over-regulating an industry. Regulations assist in protecting the environment and protecting fair practices in business, but this typically adds to the cost of doing business. There has to be balance and trade-offs between the extremes (i.e., no regulations vs. over-regulation). Each generation grapples with where the balance resides.

Demographics

What are demographics? Demographics are simply a collection of statistical data about characteristics of a population. Depending on the focus of the study, the variables or characteristics collected and evaluated as "demographic information" can fluctuate. For this text, we are interested in age, income, education, the number of births and deaths in a population, and the ethnicity of the community. How do these characteristics impact the funeral service profession and funeral rites?

The influence of the above mentioned population characteristics are correlated to the funeral service and rites in any given community. A direct relationship exists between the number of births and deaths and the funeral service industry. As populations increase, eventually more people will die and require the services of funeral service professionals.

While mortality rates affect all age categories, in the U.S. for example, the elderly population reflects a disproportionate number of deaths each year. It stands to reason that in a community with an aging population the demand for funeral services increases. That same demand decreases in communities with younger populations. In addition, as the life span increases, the opportunities for the elderly to outlive their savings also increases. This may impact the degree of services and goods purchased by this cohort. The final demographic items we consider are income, education, and ethnicity.

Income. Includes wages and salaries measured over some period, such as per hour or year (Witt, 2011). This certainly affects the prices funeral service operations as well as the funeral rites a family may choose. The connection between purchasing capacity of goods and services is obvious. Although it should be noted that higher incomes does not necessarily always equate to more elaborate funeral rites. Expenditures and income correlation is a complex issue. One should not assume a family's desires by apparent income. It is important to share all options and clearly communicate prices and payment expectations. Income inequality is an elementary characteristic of a class system (more on this in the section on social stratification and class), and as mean household incomes increase, the capacity for more extravagant funeral expenditures also increases. The obverse of this is true as well.

Education. Americans have always possessed a spirit of inquiry. The Pew Research Center confirms that Americans have attained education at record levels. In fact, a milestone was reached in 2012 when, for the first time, one-third of the age cohort from 25-29, completed at least a bachelor's degree (Fry & Parker, 2012). Informally, consumers are doing their homework outside of the classroom through powerful technological tools. Chief among these is the internet. Funeral consumers are increasingly going online to find a funeral home, read obituaries, and participate in virtual memorialization activities (NFDA Bulletin, 2010). Consider this; only 65 percent of respondents to the 2010 FAMIC Study said they would look to a funeral home or a funeral director for information on making arrangements (Lambert & Kleese, 2011). This should prompt concern among funeral service providers. The routine use of the internet by many Americans has impacted funeral service providers.

Consumers arrive at the funeral home educated, and in many cases, having already explored available cremation and memorialization options.

Funeral arrangers are well-advised to devote the requisite time to educate themselves about the available information prospective clients are accessing related to funeral goods and services (Fritch & Altieri, 2015, pg. 163). Increasing educational levels are significant in the development of a more advanced funeral consumer. Funeral service professionals must be prepared to gain the trust of clients, answer difficult questions about the industry and associated practices, and understand that many consumers are knowledgeable of competitive options.

Ethnicity. The final demographic element we consider in this section is ethnicity. An ethnic group is distinctive from others predominantly because of its national origin or distinct cultural patterns. The United States, a country founded primarily on immigration, has substantial ethnic diversity including German, Irish, Asian, English, African, Italian, Jewish, Mexican, Middle Eastern, and Latino, just to mention a few. As funeral service professionals, we must be aware that ethnic heritage may direct the choice of funeral rites. This underscores the first chapter regarding the multi-cultural reality of social life. Understanding differences in cultural traditions related to funeral practices and rituals is required for the contemporary funeral home director.

Social Stratification

Social stratification is the structured ranking of entire groups of people according to rank, caste, or class that perpetuates unequal economic rewards and power in a society. This affects industry and business. Although many would like to believe that social inequality (members of society have different amounts of wealth, prestige, or power) is minimized in the United States, the fact remains that social inequality is perpetuated in all societies, including the U.S. Social classes are outcomes or reflections of social inequality.

A class system is based on a social ranking based primarily on economic position, in which achieved characteristics can influence social mobility. In a class system, members of various classes will tend to live, shop, and socialize in these same groups. The consequence of this social pattern means that the location of a funeral home often determines the clientele it will serve. If the location is in a higher class area of the community, it will usually serve a more affluent client base. As stated previously, more personal resources to purchase funeral services often translates into purchasing the goods and services that fulfill the consumer's wishes regarding funeral rites. Conversely, a funeral home located in a poor area of the community may likely have a clientele base which struggles to afford funeral services and fall short of their expectations or wishes. For example, they may not be able to afford a traditional church service with embalming and visitation, and they are forced to select a direct cremation.

Related to stratification, inequality, and social classes is the concept of socioeconomic status, a measure of class based on income, education, occupation, and other related variables. Consistent with social class, people who are members of more affluent socioeconomic groups will typically have more resources to utilize when making funeral arrangements. This allows them to select the services, merchandise, and rites they desire. The social patterns found in the concepts of stratification, class, and socio-economic status have a profound impact on funeral rites expenditures. The funeral service profession is not immune from this reality and will experience differentiated expenditures based on capacity.

Religion

Religious beliefs and traditions (and the lack thereof) are also significant determinants of the selection of funeral rites. Religion is a set of beliefs and behavior concerning the cause, nature, and purpose of the universe, typically including sacred beliefs; it also involves devotional and ritual observances and contains a moral code of human conduct.

Religious beliefs are proclamations of a member's particular religion. How does this impact the funeral service profession? As an example, people who are raised in a faith that sanctions a religious ceremony with the deceased's body present will trigger many elements of the funeral arrangements. Religious rituals and prescriptions expected by members of a faith will often drive decisions families will make when arranging a funeral. Although the surviving spouse or children may not share the same religious beliefs of the deceased, it is commonplace for the survivor(s) to make arrangements that honor the faith of the deceased. Along with other social factors that impact the funeral service industry and the selection of funeral rites, religion and religious beliefs can play a significant role in determining the type of funeral services selected and the funeral rites desired by a client-family.

Geographic Factors

One of the geographic factors that impact the funeral industry today is the high degree of mobility. Some refer to this as neo-localism. Usage of the term is problematic because of the variegated definitions. The relevance here are the social patterns that reflect high degrees of mobility. When there are family members who live away from where the death occurs, more coordination is required between survivors and can impinge on the type of funeral services and funeral rites selected. Choosing a cemetery, whether in one's hometown, birthplace, or current residence of the deceased, are decisions that family members must make. One emerging trend is the selection of options that do not require immediate action. This may include a cremation followed by a memorial service at some future time.

In high mobile societies, survivors may likely choose funeral service options that serve their personal needs (even above the wishes of the deceased). For many, attending to funeral needs when a death occurs is declining. Collectively, this is having a serious impact on selection of funeral rites and other parts of the industry which depends on participation. Contemporary funeral service professionals should be sensitive to families searching for options that best serve their individual needs and be willing to accommodate the wishes of the family.

Chapter 4

Student Discussion Points

- Discuss the impact of economics on the funeral service industry.
- How does government policy affect the funeral service industry?
- What are demographics?
- How can a funeral home utilize demographics in business?
- What is meant by social stratification?
- What are the elements of social stratification?
- Explain the impact of religious beliefs on the funeral service industry.
- How do geographic factors impact the funeral service industry?

Chapter Five: U.S. Funeral Rites:

A Contemporary Perspective

Chapter Editor: Jamye D. Jeter Cameron, MBA, CFSP

Chapter Learning Objectives

- Examine the location of funeral rites and services in contemporary society.
- Study how the involvement of family and friends in funeral service has evolved.
- Study the advancing responsibility and roles of funeral directors.
- Acknowledge how the structure of funeral charges has changed.
- Explore the impact of technology on contemporary funeral service.
- Initiate the discussion of changing methods of disposition.
- Discuss the impact of religion and society on funeral rites.
- Discover the impact of immigration on society and funeral service.

~ U.S. FUNERAL RITES: A CONTEMPORARY PERSPECTIVE ~

As societies evolve and change, so do many funeral rites. Gone are the days of the furniture store/funeral home business establishments. Also history, is the expectation that family members and friends will care for the body of the deceased and coordinate the funeral arrangements. Except in rare cases, also gone are in home visitations, making funeral arrangements simply by selecting a casket, and assuming all families will desire the traditional services associated with burial caskets. The current expectation is that funeral directors have a wealth of knowledge regarding various cultural and societal traditions, and will be proficient when dealing with grieving families. The modern funeral director simply must be well-versed in a multitude of disciplines and, additionally, be prepared to serve as an event planner. Here, we present some funeral service practices common in the contemporary United States.

Location of Rites and Services

Preparation of remains, minimal preparation without embalming, refrigeration, and other services associated with human remains are conducted at the funeral home, centralized preparation center, or a third party mortuary service. This has not always been the case. In past generations, it was not unusual for the preparation of the remains to take place at the place of death, which was commonly in the home of the deceased.

It is no longer common practice to have a visitation or wake service in someone's home; these services are reserved for the funeral home or a church facility in the modern era. Furthermore, when considering the location of funeral rites in the contemporary United States, it is now commonplace for services to be conducted beyond the walls of a church, funeral home chapel, or the graveside. With the increasing popularity of cremation, and memorial services in general, it is now common to host funeral rites at peoples favorite social gathering place, restaurant, or school auditorium, to name but a few. Although many client families still desire funeral rites in a church, funeral home chapel, or at the graveside, with the trend toward cremation and the popularity of services without remains present, virtually any venue is now a possible option to celebrate the life well lived.

Direct Involvement of Family & Friends

With the evolvement of the funeral service industry, direct involvement of family and friends with the preparation of the deceased's body is no longer necessary or desired, except in rare cases. In modern America, it is the expectation that funeral service professionals are the ones to assist with all elements associated with human remains, especially if embalming is desired. Legal requirements necessitate one be a licensed professional embalmer or apprentice to undertake this process.

It is also true that the progression of the funeral profession has led to a reduction in the direct involvement of family and friends in coordinating funeral arrangements. When client families make arrangements with a funeral director, it is the expectation that the funeral service professional will be the one that will arrange, coordinate, and fulfill all of the desired services. This is critically important to understand; funeral service professionals must work to offer all options available to families and clearly explain the value associated with these services or clients will seek other providers. It is worthy to note, if funeral service professionals do not meet client expectations, it is trending for families to only select the services of a funeral home to arrange for the disposition of the body (direct cremation or immediate burial), and have family members, friends, and possibly a funeral coordinator assist with fulfilling the funeral rites. This is a critical reality funeral directors must remain cognizant of, and attempt to serve families in such a way that funeral directors, as service professionals, can serve the family through the entire grieving process. Without the presence of value, price is central to the decision process; the contemporary funeral professional must adequately portray and deliver the value associated with services.

The Advancing Responsibility of the Funeral Director

The responsibilities of the modern funeral director are expanding every day. It is no longer sufficient for funeral service providers to have a working knowledge of items directly related to funeral service. The current expectation is for funeral service professionals to have a solid foundation and a working knowledge of multiple disciplines including sociology, law, history, business finance, business management, and psychology, to name but a few. This allows a greater understanding of our diverse culture, and better permits funeral directors to meet the service needs of client families.

In contemporary funeral service, it is now expected that funeral professionals have an understanding of the elements of the psychology of grief and counseling in general, yet it is critical that funeral service practitioners do not actually present themselves as licensed professional counselors, unless this is indeed the case, but obtaining a working knowledge of the grief process, and counseling in general, can assist funeral directors in working with grieving families and best meet each families specific needs. In the event that families need advanced counseling services or professional mental health services, funeral service professionals should always have resources and recommendations available for clients in need of this assistance.

In the ever-changing world of funeral service, it is now expected for funeral homes and funeral directors to be prepared to assist families in planning events, not just funeral rites. Hospitality is quickly becoming an essential element in the modern service industry. Although many client families still desire, and select very traditional funeral services, the current trend is to select more personalized services including catering, video tributes, and web casting, often in a celebration/party atmosphere. Funeral service professionals must be prepared to meet such demands, or client families will go where they can receive their desired services.

The Changing Structure of Funeral Charges

At one time, it was commonplace for the price of funeral arrangements to be dictated by the cost of the casket selected; this is no longer the case. Several realities have influenced this transformation. First, the implementation of the Federal Trade Commission (FTC) Funeral Rule in 1984, required specific pricing elements, including itemization. Also, the changing funeral service environment, which offers more options and methods of disposition, reduces the need for a casket in many cases. Generally, caskets and other merchandise items are a smaller portion of the overall revenue structure of funeral homes today than in the past. As a result of changing consumer demands in funeral service and the evolving pricing structures, the overall costs emphasize charges for services rendered as opposed to merchandise selected.

The Influence of Modern Technology

Communication has never been so easy, quick, and pervasive. Although it is still most common for first contact to a funeral home after a death has occurred is via the telephone, once this contact has been made, many other modes of communication may ensue. Email, text via smartphone or tablet, video conferencing mechanisms, and social media are common methods of communication as facsimile technology is drifting into history. Funeral directors must be vigilant in the process of verifying authorized agents in this world of complex communication technologies, as it is becoming quite common for client families to communicate with funeral homes via alternative communication methods.

Web pages are now one of the most common ways that the general public learns about different funeral homes, the merchandise and services they offer, and the prices for these items. It is becoming increasingly important for funeral homes to have inviting, professional websites that communicate the culture, atmosphere, and mission of the funeral home. How a potential client feels about a funeral home after visiting their website may indeed be the factor that ultimately decides which funeral home to select at the time of need. These elements must be considered when funeral homes develop business and marketing plans, if they intend to remain relevant in the contemporary business environment. In the modern era, web presence may provide a funeral home's first impression. Therefore, websites must be user friendly, easy to understand, informational, and communicate the culture of the funeral establishment.

Additional impacts of the internet include virtual guest books for family and friends to sign online, online obituaries, the development of virtual memorials online, the practice of webcasting funeral services, and even offering drive through visitation (viewing of remains via a monitor available as people never get out of their car). This is not your parents' industry; contemporary society presents more challenges and opportunities than any time in history, especially when you consider technology!

Transportation is another area that has been significantly impacted by modern technology. With an extensive interstate highway system, high speed rail, and pervasive air travel opportunities, it seems people can be across the country or world in record time. Not only does this mean client families can make arrangements from across the world via the internet one day and attend a service the next day, it also means multiple methods exist for transporting human remains if the death occurs in an area other than the desired place of final rest. As a result of the vast impacts of technology, and specifically on transportation, the world of the modern funeral director is smaller than ever before, and the professional funeral director must be a wealth of knowledge for client families that need assistance and recommendations regarding transportation.

Changing Methods of Disposition

Yes, we still see traditional church, garden, and memorial park style cemeteries, but the modern cemetery continues to evolve. It is now common for cemeteries to offer mausoleums and, with the increasing rates of cremation, columbarium niches. If cemeteries do not offer many of these options, people will simply go elsewhere, especially when considering niches for cremated remains, as many churches and even some funeral homes offer columbarium niches for the permanent placement of cremated remains. Other contemporary options include cremation-only cemeteries utilizing GPS technology to locate remains, as well as scattering gardens and ossuaries for the commingling of cremated remains. As modern society is becoming more aware of the need for environmental conservation, the development of "Green" cemeteries is also an aspect of our industry we need to be aware of, as these cemeteries have specific requirements (for example, no embalming, and specific container and marker requirements) that will influence the goods and services we offer to client families.

It is time to embrace the cremation revolution; the rate of cremation was projected to exceed the rate of burial in the United States for the first time in 2015, as predicted by the Cremation Association of North America (CANA) and the National Funeral Directors Association (NFDA). The increase in cremation is arguably the most significant factor in changing funeral rites in the United States. When cremation is selected, more options are available, and time is not of the essence, as the initial disposition of the body has been completed.

Other options when dealing with human remains include body donation, immediate burial, entombment and alkaline hydrolysis. In order to remain germane in the industry, funeral service professionals must remain familiar with the various options available and be prepared to offer services and merchandise to serve and support families that select different options. We must remember that if we do not serve the demands of our customers, someone else will.

Funeral Rites – The Impact of Religion & Society

The disposition of human remains and the associated rites and pageantry is considered by many to be one of the oldest historical traditions. Many times the rites have deep connections to religious, spiritual, and/or cultural traditions, and these connections, no doubt, determine the actual rites and services desired by the surviving family and the greater community. Multiple books have been dedicated to the exploration of various religious and social traditions considering burial rites. This is beyond the scope of this text. Our goal here is to acknowledge the impact of religion and society on funeral rites and identify five classifications used to describe the types of services planned in contemporary society. Many rudiments drive the specific funeral rites selected by client families. The five common classifications associated with this practice include the following.

Traditional Funeral Rites: Funeral rites that adhere to specific rituals or ceremonies. It is common for these rites to be dictated by faith orientation, religious beliefs, or social customs.

Adaptive Funeral Rites: Funeral rites that have been modified to meet the current needs of the surviving family and friends. These rites have been transformed to better suit current social trends.

Humanistic Funeral Rites: Funeral rites lacking religious connotations.

Immediate Disposition: The disposition of human remains without any form of funeral rite at the time of disposition.

Non-Traditional Funeral Rites: Any funeral rites that stray from what is considered "normal" or the established custom of the culture or community.

The Impact of Immigration

The Unites States, a country developed by immigrants, continues to be influenced by this reality. Historically referred to as the great "melting pot" because of the great number of countries and cultures represented in its population, the Unites States is growing more diverse over time. The direct impact on the funeral service industry is the need to study and understand the various cultures of the people we serve in order to build rapport and trusted relationships, as well as to be more prepared to meet their service needs. The more we understand about our clients, and why they desire specific services, the better we will be able to serve these families. This reality is consistent with the statements above regarding the increasing requirements of funeral directors in the contemporary business environment, including an understanding of the social sciences. It is the duty and responsibility of funeral service providers to be familiar with, and understand the cultures and service needs of the diverse clients they have the honor to serve, as immigration is continual, funeral service professionals must work to remain knowledgeable of their diverse community and changing culture. This reality reinforces the value and importance of Sociology as related to the funeral service profession.

Chapter 5

Student Discussion Points

- How has the location and type of funeral rites changed in contemporary society?
- What has been the evolution of direct involvement of family and friends in funeral arrangements?
- How has the role and expectations of the contemporary funeral director changed over time?
- How has the funeral service pricing structure changed?
- Explain the influence of technology in funeral service.
- Discuss various methods of disposition.
- What are the five common classifications of funeral rites?
- Discuss the impact of immigration on society and specifically on the funeral service industry.

Adaptive Funeral Rite: Funeral rite adjusted to the needs and desires of the family or the trends of the times.

Adaptive Strategy: A society's system of economic production (economy).

Agrarian: Related to land, land tenure, agriculture, or the division of landed property.

Agrarian Society: The most technologically advanced form of preindustrial society. Members are engaged primarily in the production of food, but they see increases in crop yield through basic technological innovations.

Anonymity: The quality or state of being unknown to most people: the quality or state of being anonymous. When a person or entity is unknown.

Blended Family: A family unit consisting of one male and one female, their children together, and any children they each may have from previous marriages or relationships

Bureaucratization: A method of administrative system governing any large institution, be it public or private. Bureaucratic institutions are enduring and impersonal in asserting and sustaining power.

Ceremony (Ritual): An established or prescribed procedure for a religious or other rite; the formal activities conducted on some solemn or important occasion.

Class: A group of people who have a similar level of economic resources.

Cohabitants: The practice of two unrelated adults of the opposite sex living together without being married.

Contemporary: Living or occurring at the same time; belonging to or occurring in the present.

Cultural Relativism: The viewing of people's behavior from the perspective of their own culture.

Cultural Shock: The feelings of disorientation, uncertainty, and even fear that people experience when they encounter unfamiliar cultural practices.

Cultural Universal: A common practice or belief shared by all societies.

Culture: The totality of our shared language, knowledge, material objects, and behavior.

Customs: An action or behavior in line with tradition of a particular group or place, consistent with the tradition of the people.

Demographics: a collection of statistical data about characteristics of a population.

Diffusion: The process by which a cultural item spreads from group to group or society to society.

Direct Learning (Formal): Attaining culture through deliberate instruction by other members of that society.

Division of Labor: A production process in which a worker or group of workers is assigned a specialized task in order to increase efficiency.

Egalitarian: An authority pattern in which spouses are regarded as equals.

Enculturation (Socialization): The lifelong process through which people learn the attitudes, values, and behaviors appropriate for members of a particular culture.

Ethnic Group: A group that is set apart from others, primarily because of its national origin or distinctive cultural patterns.

Ethnocentrism: The tendency to assume that one's own culture and way of life represents what's normal or are superior to all others.

Extended Family: A family in which relatives, such as grandparents, aunts, or uncles, live in the same household as parents and their children.

Folkways: Norms governing everyday behavior, whose violation raises comparatively little concern.

Funeral (Funeral Service): Rites performed with the body present.

Funeral Rite: An all-inclusive term that represents all funerals and/or memorial services.

Globalization: The worldwide integration of government policies, cultures, social movements, and financial markets through trade and the exchange of ideas.

Hospitality: The contemporary practice in funeral service that includes the friendly and generous reception and entertainment of guests.

Humanistic Funeral Rite: Funeral rites lacking religious connotations.

Immediate Disposition: The disposition of human remains without any form of funeral rite at the time of disposition.

Immutability: The stability/order characteristic of a society; societies resist change.

Indirect Learning (Informal): Attaining culture through observation of other members of that society.

Industrialization: The process by which a society transforms from a primarily agricultural adaptive strategy (economy) to the manufacturing of goods and services through advanced technical enterprises.

Innovation: The process of introducing a new idea or object to a culture through discovery or invention.

Law: Formal norms enforced by the state.

Matriarchal: A society in which women dominate in family decision making.

Memorial Service: A funeral rite conducted without the body present.

Mobility: The ability to move or be moved freely and easily; the state or quality of being mobile; ability to migrate about social classes.

Modified Extended Family: Household or family unit formed by two or more nuclear families or friendships.

Mores: Norms deemed highly necessary to the welfare of a society.

Multicultural: Of, relating to, or constituting several cultural or ethnic groups within a society.

Neo-localism: Renewed interest in preserving and promoting the identity of a community and restoring aspects that make it culturally unique or the movement of families away from where they were born and raised.

Non-Traditional Funeral Rite: Funeral rite that deviates from the normal or established custom.

Norms: An established standard of behavior maintained by a society.

Nuclear family: A married couple and their unmarried children living together.

Patriarchal: A society in which men dominate in family decision making.

Pre-literate Society: Of, related to, or being a culture not having a written language.

Post-Industrialization: A society whose economic system is engaged primarily in the processing and control of information.

Religion: A culturally embedded configuration of behavior made up of sacred beliefs, emotional feelings accompanying the beliefs, and overt behavior seemingly executing the beliefs and feelings.

Religious Ritual: A practice required or expected of members of faith.

Rite: A religious, cultural, social, or other solemn ceremony or act.

Rites of Passage: A ritual marking the symbolic transition from one social position to another.

Ritual: An established or prescribed procedure for a religious or other rite; the formal activities conducted on some solemn or important occasion.

Rules: A set of explicit or understood regulations or principles governing conduct within a particular sphere.

Rural: Of or related to the countryside rather than the town.

Single Parent Family: A family in which only one parent is present to care for the children.

Social: Of or related to society or its organization.

Social Anonymity: People are relatively unknown to the larger community

Social Dynamics: Those elements of society that impact change.

Social Institution: An organized pattern of beliefs and behavior centered on basic social needs.

Social Function: An event that allows people to share something of which they have in common.

Social Mobility: Movement of individuals or groups from one position in a society's stratification system to another.

Social Stratification: The structured ranking of entire groups of people according to rank, caste, or class that perpetuates unequal economic rewards and power in a society.

Socialization: The lifelong process through which people learn attitudes, values, and behaviors appropriate for members of a particular culture.

Society: The structure of relationships within which culture is created and shared through regularized patterns of social interaction.

Sociobiology: The systematic study of the relationships between the individual and society and of the consequences of difference.

Sociology: The systematic study of the relationship between the individual and society and of the consequences of difference.

Statuses: Social positions we occupy relative to others.

Subculture: A segment of society that shares distinctive pattern of mores, folkways, and values that differs from the pattern of the larger society.

Symbol: A gesture, object, or word that forms the basis of human communication.

Taboos: Prohibited or restricted by social custom.

Traditional Funeral Rite: A funeral rite that follows a prescribed social or religious ritual or ceremony.

Urbanization: Living patterns that reflect a high density of people in a relatively bounded space.

Values: A collective conception of what is considered good, desirable, and proper (or bad, undesirable, and improper) in a culture.

Benokraitis, Nijole V. 2014. Soc Third edition. Belmont, CA: Wadsworth.

Cremation Association of North America, http://www.cremationassociation.org/

Centers for Disease Control. *National Vital Statistics Report (NVSR)Deaths: Final Data for 2011*. Retrieved from http://www.cdc.gov/nchs/data/nvsr/nvsr63/ nvsr63_03.pdf

Cooley, Charles H. 1909. Social Organization: The Study of the Larger Mind. New York: Charles Scribner's Sons.

Corr, C.A., & Corr, D.M. (2013). *Death and dying, life and living* (7th ed.), Belmont, CA: Wadsworth.

Durkheim, E. (1964, orig. 1893). *The Division of Labor in Society*. New York: Free Press.

Fritch, J.B., & Altieri, J.C. (2015). *Fires of change: A comprehensive examination of cremation*, Oklahoma City, OK: Funeral Service Education Resource Center.

Fry, R., & Parker, K. (2012, November 5). *Record Shares of Young Adults Have Finished Both High School and College*. Retrieved from Pew Research Center Social Trends website: http://www.pewsocialtrends.org/2012/11/05/record-shares-of-young-adults-have-finished-both-high-school-and-college/#overview

International Council on Active Aging. (2009). *The Business Case for Wellness Programs in Retirement Communities and Seniors Housing, A white paper*. Retrieved from http://www.icaa.cc/business/whitepapers/ icaabusinesscase-wp.pdf

Kastenbaum, R.J. (2008). *Death, society, and human experience.* (9th ed.), Boston, MA: Pearson Education, Inc.

Lambert, D., & Kleese, P. (2011). FAMIC Research Reveals Opportunities and Threats. Retrieved from http://www.homesteaderslife.com/userdocs/FAMIC-Opportunities_Threats.pdf

Macionis, John J. 2008. Sociology. (12th ed.), Upper   Saddle River, NJ: Pearson Education, Inc.

Mansfield, E. & Behravesh, N. (1998). *Economics USA.* (5th ed.), New York, NY: W.W. Norton & Company, Inc.

National Funeral Directors Association. (2014, September). *The NFDA Cremation and Burial Report: Research, Statistics and Projections*. Retrieved from http://nfda.org/surveys-a-reports-businessmangement/cat_view/223-other-documents/240-cremation.html

Professional Training Schools, Inc. (2002). *Sociology for funeral service.*(3rd ed.), Dallas, TX: Professional Training Schools Inc.

Ritzer, G. (2013). *Introduction to sociology.* Thousand Oaks, CA: Sage Publications.

Schlesinger, R. (2011) . "Two Takes: Collective Bargaining Rights for Public Sector Unions?" U.S. News Weekly, February 25, 15-16.

Sumner, W.G. (1940, orig.1906). *Folkways,* New York: Dover

Tonnies, F. (1963,orig. 1887). *Community and Society: (Gemeinschaft and Gesellschaft).* New York: Harper and Row.

Turner, Jonathan H., Leonard Beeghley, and Charles H. Powers. 1989. The Emergence of Sociological Theory. Second edition. Belmont: Wadsworth Publishing Company.

Weber, M. (1978, orig. 1921). *Economy and Society: An outline of interpretive sociology.* Guenther Roth and Claus Wittich, eds. Berkeley: University of California Press.

Witt, J. (2011). *Soc* (2nd ed.), New York, NY: McGraw Hill

Sociology & Funeral Service: Index

A

Adaptive Funeral
Rite: 62, 65
Adaptive
Strategy: 21, 23,
65, 68
Agrarian: 21, 22,
27, 65
Agrarian Society:
65
Anonymity: 65

B

Blended Family:
38, 65
Bureaucratization
21, 65

C

Ceremony: 5, 11,
14, 16, 34, 51,
65, 70, 71
Class: 7, 8, 22,
23, 38, 48, 49,
50, 51, 65
Cohabitants: 39,
66
Cultural
Relativism: 16,
66
Cultural Shock:
66
Cultural
Universal: 16,
34, 66

D

Demographics:
4, 47, 66
Diffusion: 16, 66
Direct Learning:
66
Division of
Labor: 22, 66

E

Egalitarian: 36,
67
Enculturation:
12, 14, 67
Ethnic Group:
41, 49, 67
Ethnocentrism:
16, 67
Extended Family:
11, 37, 38, 67

F

Folkways: 8
Funeral Rite: 12,
33, 34, 35, 39,
40, 41, 44, 47,
48, 49, 50, 51,
52, 55, 56, 57,
58, 61, 62, 63,
65, 67, 68, 69, 71

G

Globalization: 2,
3, 67

H

Hospitality: 58,
67
Humanistic
Funeral Rite: 63,
68

I

Immediate
Disposition: 63,
68
Immutability: 4,
68
Indirect
Learning: 68
Industrialization:
21, 22, 24, 68
Innovation: 16,
68

L

Law: 6, 8, 27,
35, 40, 46, 57, 68

M

Matriarchal: 36,
68
Memorial
Service: 15, 33,
52, 56, 67, 68
Mobility: 3, 50,
52, 68

NOTES